meet the family
my Aunt and Uncle

by Mary Auld

W
FRANKLIN WATTS
LONDON • SYDNEY

This is Nell and her brother Simon with their Aunt Sue and Uncle Clive. Sue is their dad's sister and Clive is her husband.

Paul and Dina's mum has a younger brother, Anthony. He is Paul and Dina's uncle. Paul is Anthony's nephew. Dina is his niece.

Will has four aunts and seven uncles! Here they all are with Will's mum.

Stella's Auntie Christine isn't related to her at all — she is her mum's best friend.

Oliver's uncle
often babysits
when his parents
go out.

Rob's uncle runs
his own business.

Shanti's
aunt
is a
student.

Duncan's aunt takes her
nephew out for a treat.

Clarice's uncle and aunt taught her to ride a bike.

Alice and Penny
go on holiday
with their uncle
and aunt.

Rob likes talking to his aunt about all sorts of things.

Lucy likes playing with her cousins – the children of her aunts and uncles.

This is Tom with his dad and his dad's uncle and aunt, Tom's Great-uncle Jack and Great-aunt Naomi.

Do you have an aunt or uncle?
What are they like?

Family words

Here are some words people use when talking about their aunts, uncles or family.

Uncle; Aunt, Auntie; Nephew, Niece.

Names for parents:
Father, Daddy, Dad, Pa;
Mother, Mummy, Mum, Ma.

Names of other relatives:
Sister, Brother; Daughter, Son;
Grandchildren; Grandparents;
Gran, Granny, Grandma, Grandmother;
Grandad, Grandpa, Grandfather.

If we put the word 'great' in front of a relative's name it means that they are separated from us by an extra generation of family. Look at the family tree on page 24; each level on it is a generation.

A family tree

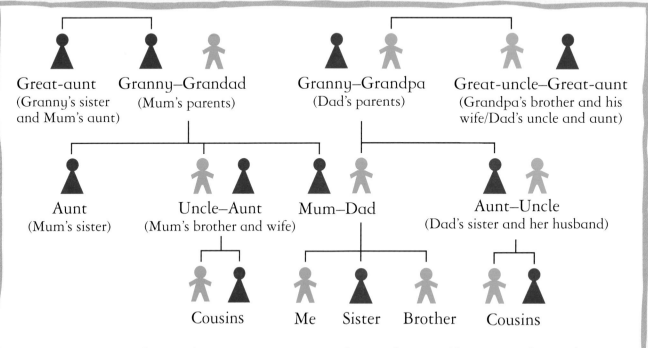

Great-aunt (Granny's sister and Mum's aunt) — Granny–Grandad (Mum's parents) — Granny–Grandpa (Dad's parents) — Great-uncle–Great-aunt (Grandpa's brother and his wife/Dad's uncle and aunt)

Aunt (Mum's sister) — Uncle–Aunt (Mum's brother and wife) — Mum–Dad — Aunt–Uncle (Dad's sister and her husband)

Cousins — Me — Sister — Brother — Cousins

You can show how you are related to all your family on a plan like this one. It is called a family tree. Every family tree is different. Try drawing your own.

First published in 2003 by Franklin Watts, 96 Leonard Street, London EC2A 4XD

Franklin Watts Australia 45-51 Huntley Street, Alexandria, NSW 2015

Copyright © Franklin Watts 2003

Series editor: Rachel Cooke
Art director: Jonathan Hair
Design: Andrew Crowson

A CIP catalogue record for this book is available from the British Library.

ISBN 0 7496 5116 4

Printed in Hong Kong/China

Acknowledgements:
Bruce Berman/Corbis: front cover centre. www.johnbirdsall.co.uk: front cover centre below, 1, 6, 9, 15, 18, 19. Jackie Chapman/Photofusion: 13. Carlos Goldin/Corbis: front cover centre above. Sally Greenhill/Sally & Richard Greenhill PL: 16-17. Judy Harrison/Format: 10. David Montford/Photofusion: 2. Jose Luis Pelaez/Corbis: front cover top. Ulrike Preuss/Format: 14. David Raymer/Corbis: 12. George Shelley/Corbis: front cover bottom, 5. Ariel Skelley/Corbis: front cover main, 22. Jeff Zaruba Studio/Corbis: 20-21.

Whilst every attempt has been made to clear copyright should there be any inadvertent omission please apply in the first instance to the publisher regarding rectification.